KNITTING FOR BEGINNERS

A Complete step by step guide with picture illustrations to learn how to knit with awesome knitting projects to make

Mary Gilbert

copyright@2021

Table of content

CHAPTER ONE

INSTRUCTIONS TO KNITING FOR BEGINNERS

This guide will show you all you require to begin with weaving.

To begin with, you'll figure out how to get yarn onto the needles. At that point, you'll figure out how to make the significant knit stitch. Finally, we'll turn out how to get your stitch off the needles. Weaving is as easy as 1, 2, 3

Weaving is made up of three fundamental abilities. These are the cast on, sew stitch, and the cast off. These three strategies make up the foundation of weaving. Learn them and you're confidently a knitter. It's that straightforward!

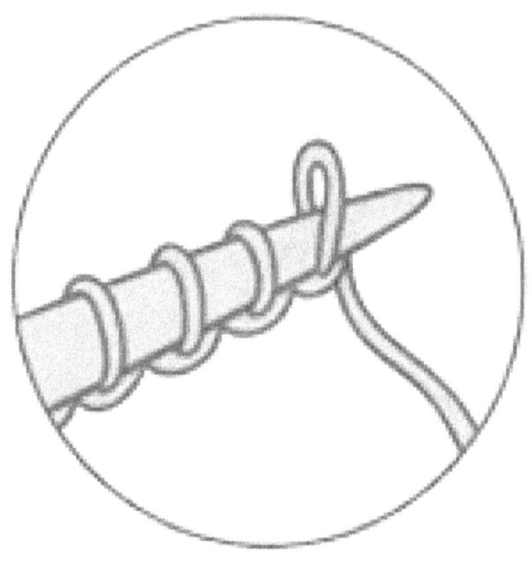

1. Cast On

The experience starts! Change free yarn into slick join.

2. Sew Stitch

This straightforward join makes up the foundation of sewing.

3. Cast Off

Get your weaving off the needles so you can wear it and pleased!

Before You Begin:

Gather Your materials[supplies]

To sew, you'll need needles and yarn. That is it! In any case, where to get them? Also, what sort of needles and yarn? Thick or meager? Wood or plastic? The alternatives are unending!

❖ YARN: I generally suggest a stout yarn and correspondingly thick needles for tenderfoots since they're a lot simpler to grasp.

In these instructional exercises I'm utilizing Lion Brand's Hometown (in shading Fort Lauderdale Coral) and 9mm needles.

You don't have to utilize a similar yarn as me, however attempt to get yarn that is in any event a medium weight (otherwise known as. worsted weight) or thicker. More slender yarns are more earnestly to control. Not certain what "yarn weight" is? Look at this concise manual for yarn loads.

Excessively cumbersome acrylic yarn by Lion Brand Hometown USA 10mm bamboo needles

TIP: If you're purchasing yarn and needles, pick modest acrylic yarn so that errors won't feel like a particularly serious deal. As a learner, you'll commit errors – and that is absolutely typical!

Mix-ups are important for the excursion, and they'll hurt less in case you're utilizing modest yarn rather than expensive craftsman yarn.

- ❖ NEEDLES: I suggest wood or bamboo needles for fledglings. Wood and bamboo have a characteristic surface drag that "holds" the yarn and make it less elusive than steel or aluminum needles. Plastic needles are OK as well.

On the off chance that you have the decision, go for bamboo or wood. Something else, utilize anything that's accessible!

- ❖ SIZE of needle needed: What needle size do you need? It relies upon the yarn you use! At the point when you purchase a wad of yarn, the yarn mark will ordinarily incorporate a "suggested needle size" recorded in millimeters.

Follow the yarn name when you're first beginning. Going up or down a millimeter won't be serious, however any more and your weaving may be excessively close or excessively free.

Most yarn names will incorporate a suggested needle size. On this name, a 9mm needle is suggested.

CHAPTER TWO

CAST ON

You have needles and a wad of yarn. Presently you need to sew something. In any case, how would you get the yarn onto your needles? Enter the cast on!

Projecting on is an approach to transform free yarn into slick little fastens that sit entirely on your needle. It's the initial phase in sewing. Watch the video for a full bit by bit instructional exercise or track with in 12 stages beneath. Prepared to begin? How about we do this!

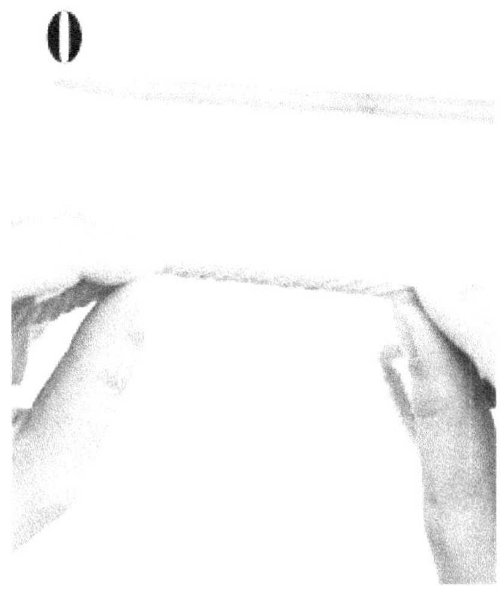

Leave a liberal yarn tail and squeeze yarn
with two hands

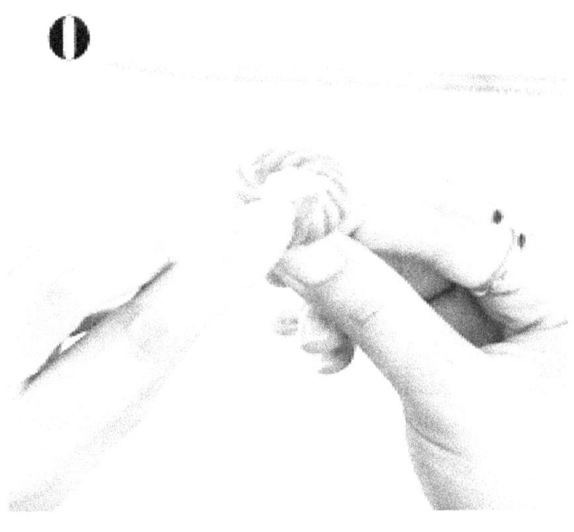

Hold the yarn and unite the hands to make a circle

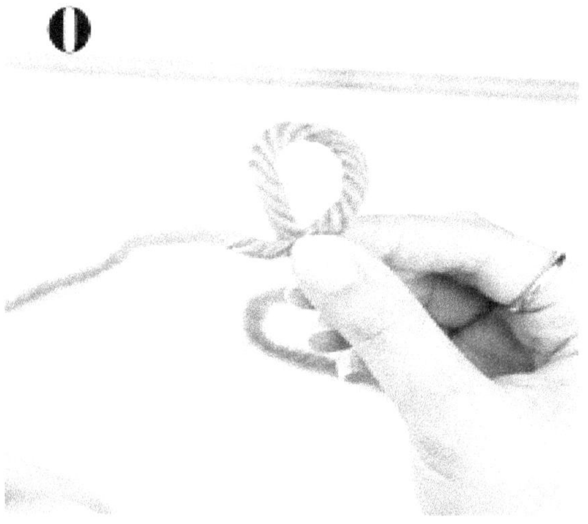

 Hold the circle that you have made in one hand

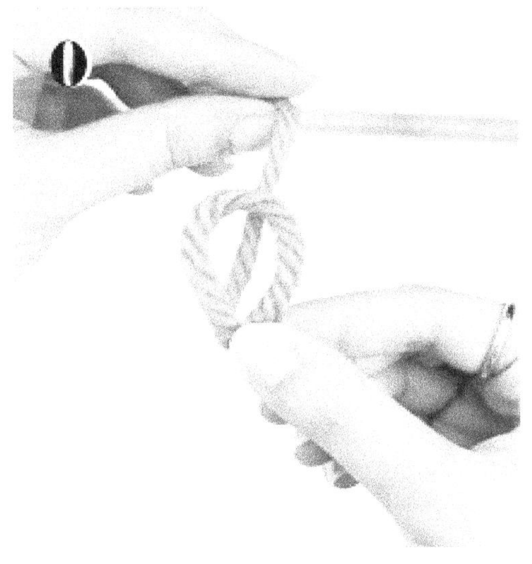

Grab the yarn that is unattached to the ball and bring it behind the circle

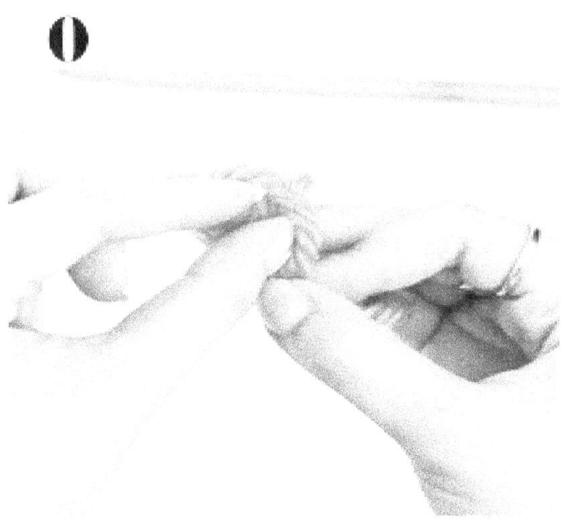

Pull the strand of yarn through the circle

This little circle is known as a slipknot.
Your're prepared to project on with it!

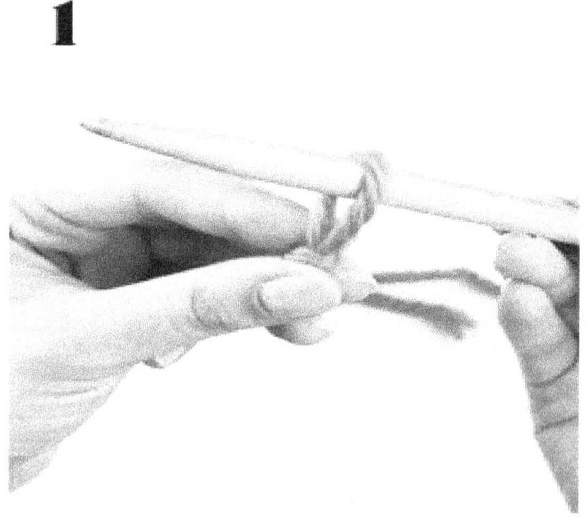

Spot a slipknot on the needle and pull yarn
tails to tighten

Grab the short yarn tail and offer a thumps
up

3

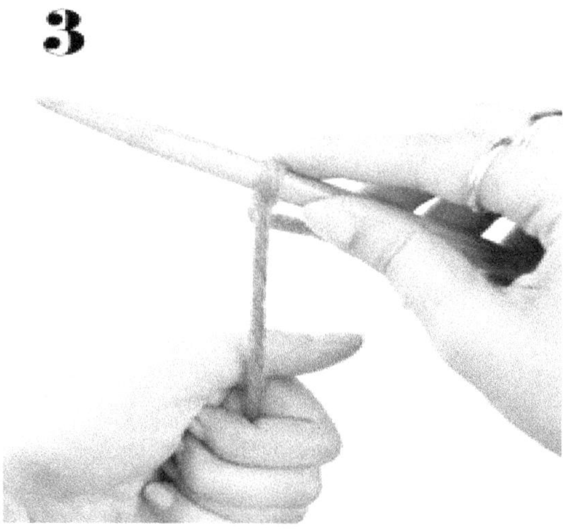

Swing the thumb behind the yarn

4

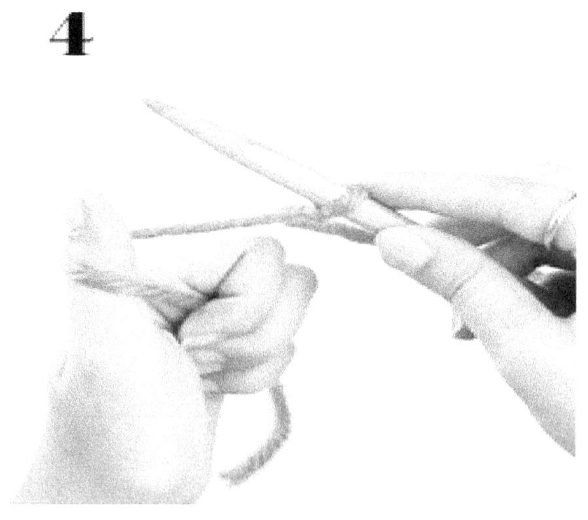

 Hook the yarn onto your thumb. Keep a strong hold!

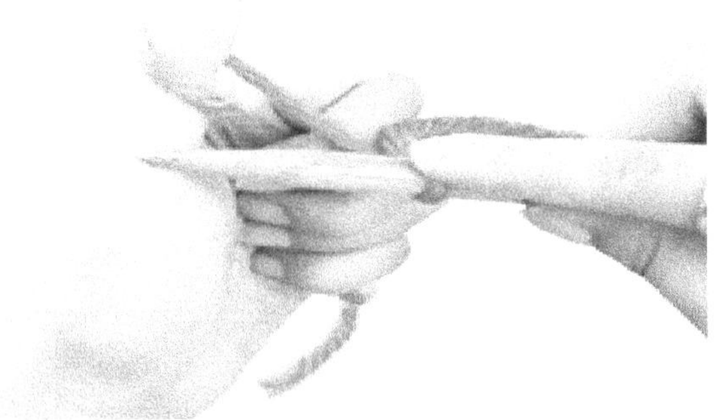

Contact the needle to the front of the thumb… …

6

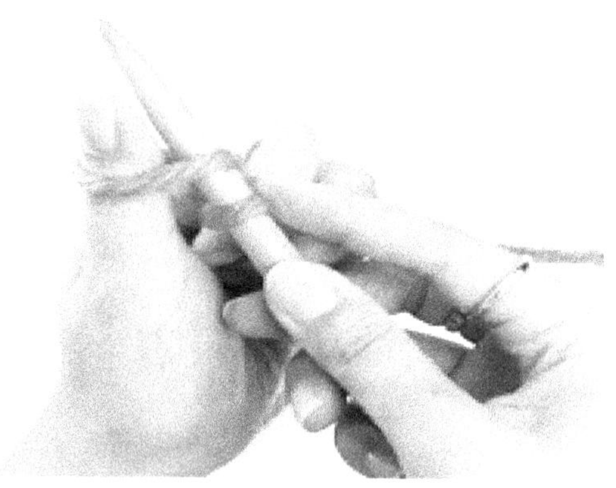

 and slide the needle into the circle on your thumb

7

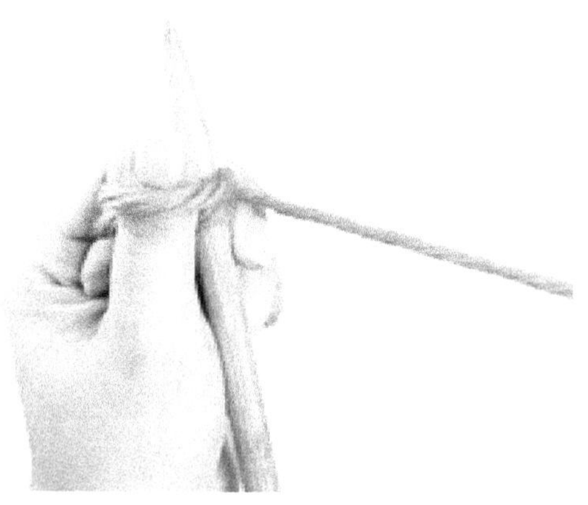

Hold the needle and snatch the yarn joined
to the ball with right hand Wrap the yarn
around the needle, from back to front

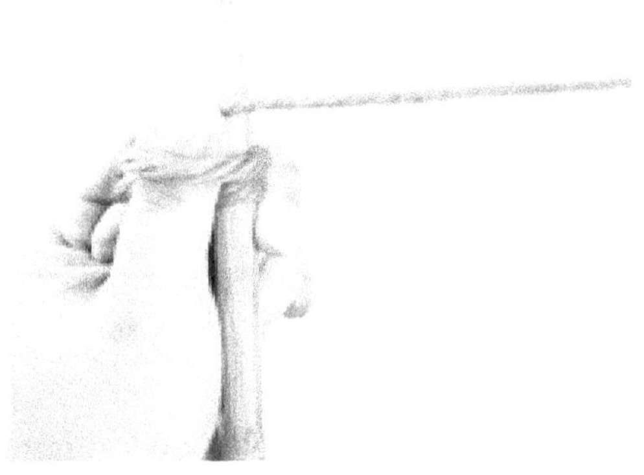

9

Pull down the yarn so it meets the circle on
the thumb

10

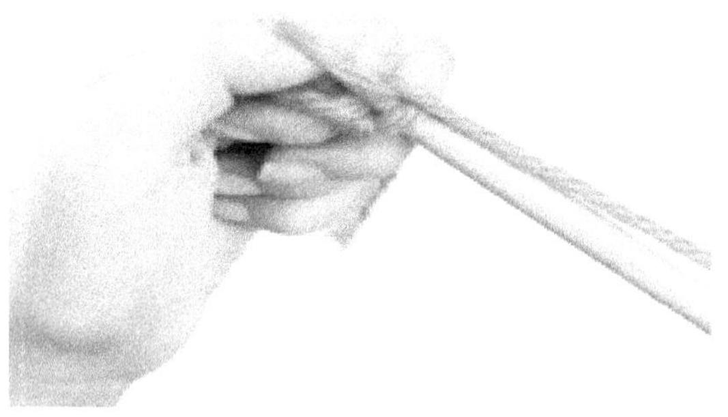

Pull the circle on your thumb over the needle.

Place the circle on the needle

Pull down the yarn tail to fix the new join!
Repeat stages 2-12

Knit Stitch

You've figured out how to transform yarn into fastens – great job! Be that as it may, they can't simply stay there like knocks on a log. They're holding on to be weave!

The weave line is the most essential and central fasten. All things considered, it's the namesake of the art we're learning. Expert the weave fasten and you, old buddy, are a bonafide knitter.

1

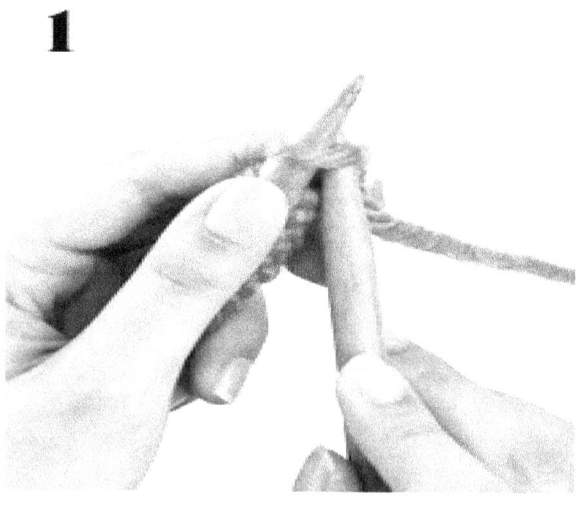

Addition right needle into first join, base to top

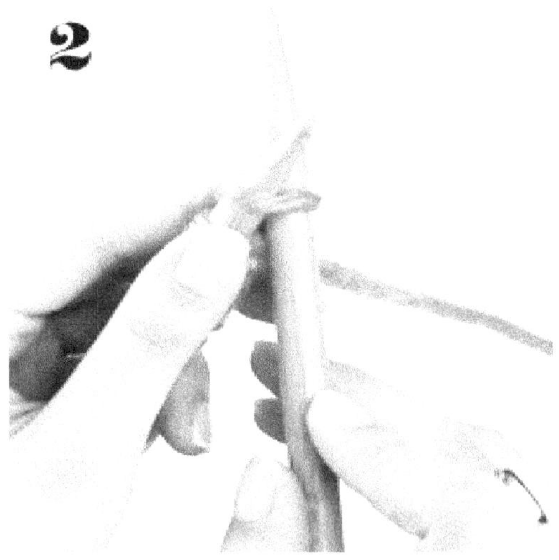

Push right needle into the stitch

Grab the yarn appended to the bundle of yarn

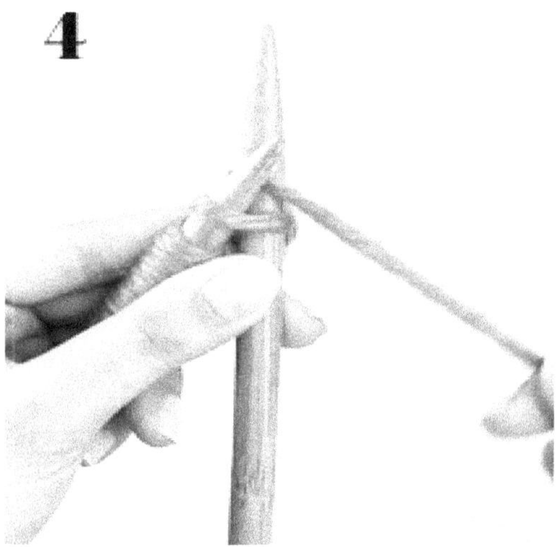

Use the yarn to Wrap around the needle, back to front

5

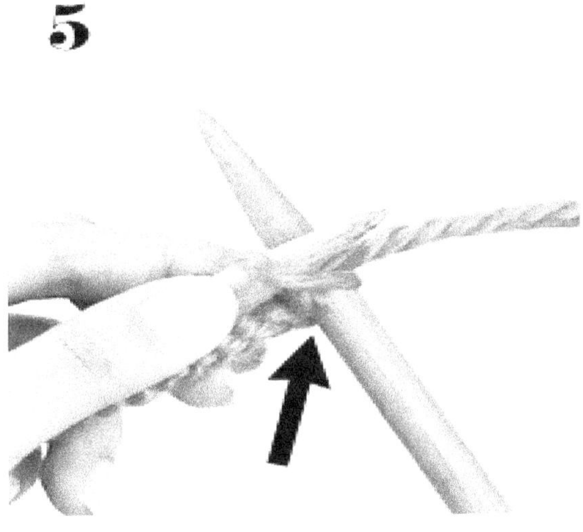

Pull yarn down and notice the yarn looks
through the stitch

6

Gently pull the needle down and select the yarn on the needle

7

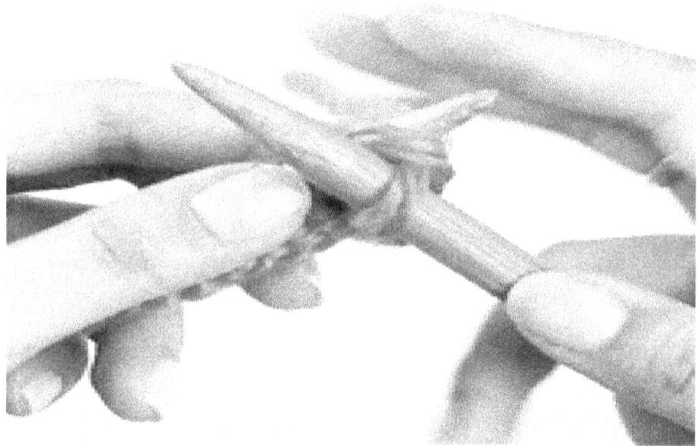

Push the correct needle into the circle. This is another stitch

8

Pull the correct needle off the left needle

9

Pull yarn joined to chunk of yarn to fix line.

Repeat stages 1-9

Please note: Like most aptitudes, sewing sets aside some effort to consummate. You most likely won't get the hang of it on your first attempt. You presumably won't get it on your subsequent attempt. The significant thing is to continue to attempt.

Why?

You've heard the idea of "muscle memory," correct? The thought the more you rehash a development, the more it turns out to be natural.

Since the development is constrained by your psyche mind rather than your cognizant brain, you don't have to thoroughly consider each progression of a development. Without speculation, you can take care of business. That is muscle memory!

At the point when you first beginning sewing, your hands will feel huge and ungainly holding those sewing needles. Yet, in the wake of rehearsing, your hands will become familiar with the development of weaving. It's practically similar to your hands have their own cerebrum!

Consider it like figuring out how to drive. As another driver, you presumably focused truly hard on the most proficient method to turn the wheel. It is safe to say that you are turning excessively hard? Will you hit the check? Goodness my gosh, the light turned yellow. Hit the brake!

You're an apprehensive, sweat-soaked wreck. In any case, with training, you figured out the amount to transform the haggle to slip into a stop so you don't get whiplash. Sooner or later, driving turns out to be natural. Your hands and feet sort out some way to facilitate with your eyes and mind to move your vehicle around – no simple accomplishment! That is the marvel of muscle memory.

Along these lines, don't worry on the off chance that you don't move the weave fasten immediately. A great many people don't. The more you practice, the quicker muscle memory will kick in. Before you know it, you'll be sewing with your eyes shut.!

Turn Me Right Round

Here's some sewing jargon for you: those cast on lines on your needle? That is known as a ROW. Or on the other hand more explicitly, a line of fastens.

At the point when you've sew all the fastens on your needle, that implies you've weave the entire line. Woohoo! That is serious!

What happens next!

OK, notice that after you've finished your column, the yarn is at the left half of your line (otherwise known as. the finish of your line). To continue to weave, you need the yarn at the correct side of the line (otherwise known as. the start of the line).

How to do this?

It couldn't be simpler! Simply turn the needle around. Ta-da! The working yarn (otherwise known as. the yarn connected to the ball) is currently at the correct side of the line, and you have another column of lines, prepared to be sew!

Each time you get to the furthest limit of the column, simply turn your work around so the working yarn is on the right. Continue going until your sewing is the length of you need it to be.

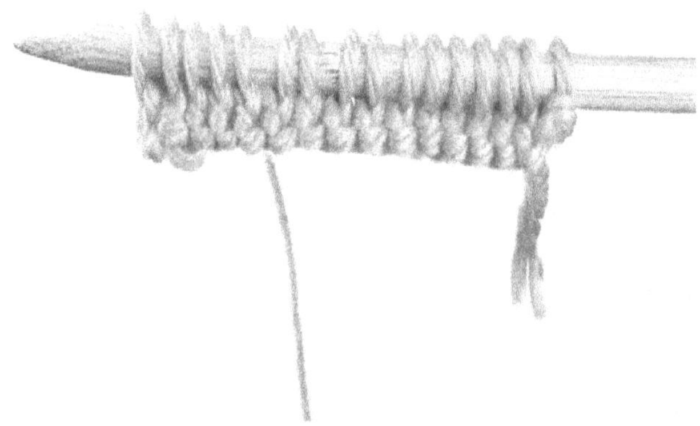

Toward the finish of the line, your needle will confront left.

Turn the needle around with the goal that it faces the privilege

3

The needle currently faces the right. Get the exposed needle and keep knitting

CHAPTER THREE

CAST OFF

Now, you have a few lines of weaving added to your sleeves. You ought to be pleased with yourself! You've utilized two sticks to change a free heap of string into a slick little square shape. Stunning! Presently it's an ideal opportunity to get your weaving off the needles. The cast off will take care of business. This method is magnificent on the grounds that it implies that your undertaking is finished! It's full grown, prepared to take off the needles and enter this present reality!

HOT TIP: When pushing off, recollect that you generally need TWO STITCHES on the correct needle to push off. No more and no less. Pushing off is a game for two (join).

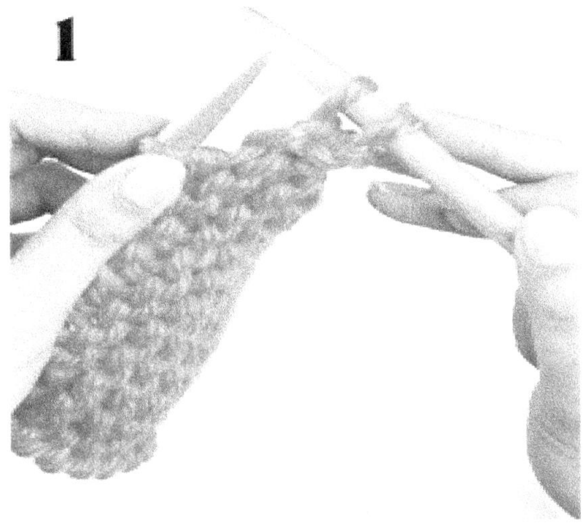

Sew two fastens

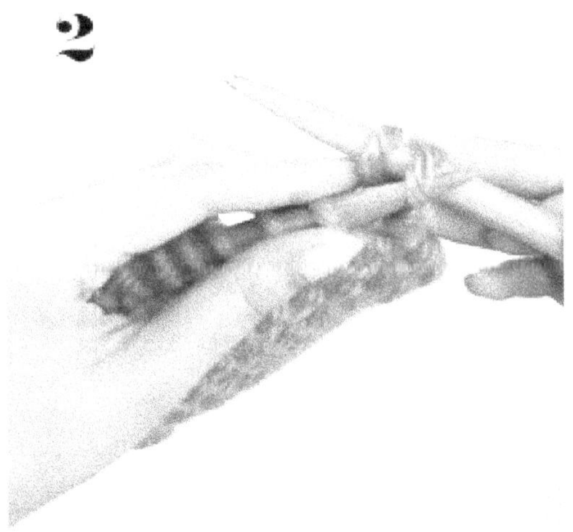

Slide left needle into first stitch

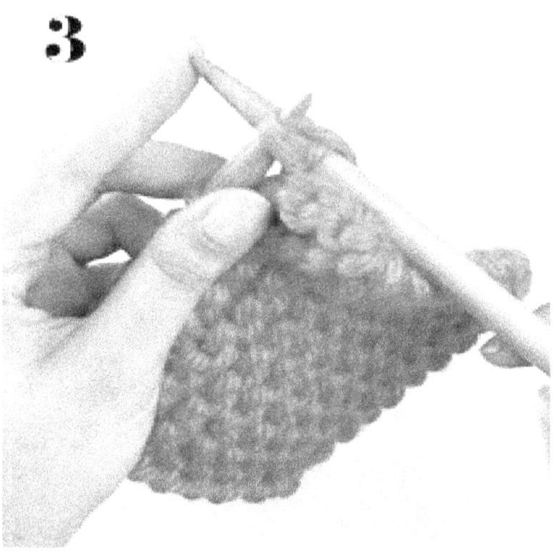

Pull the main join throughout the subsequent stitch

Continue to pull the primary line over the course of the subsequent stitch and off the needle

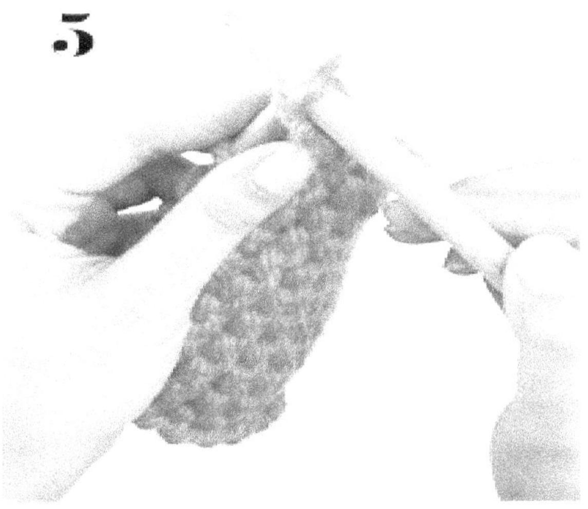

There is currently one line on the correct needle. Different has been pushed off!

8

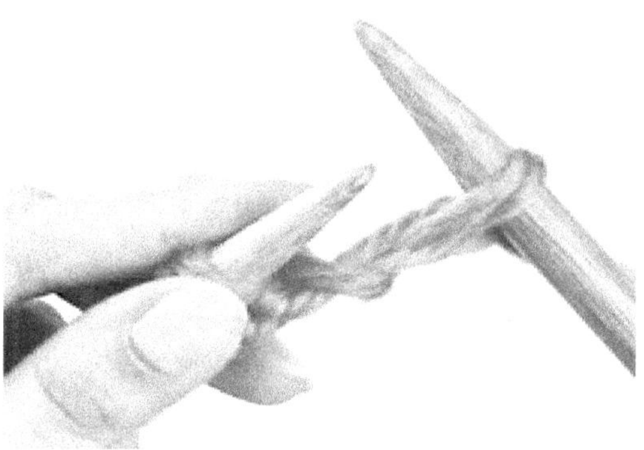

Sew one join. Rehash Steps 2-6 until one line remains

7

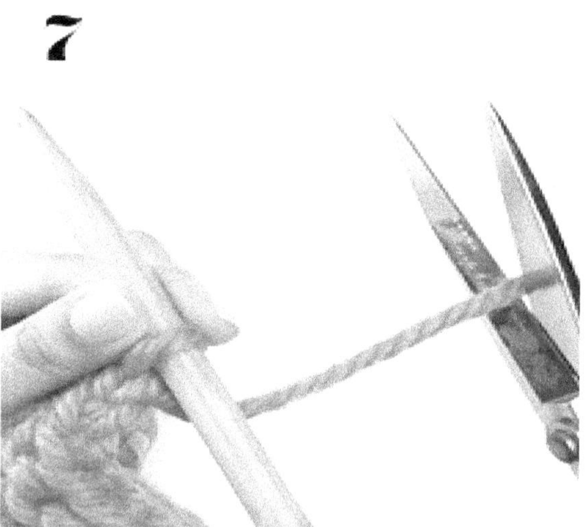

 When one stitch stay, remove a 10" yarn tail

8

Wrap the yarn around the needle

9

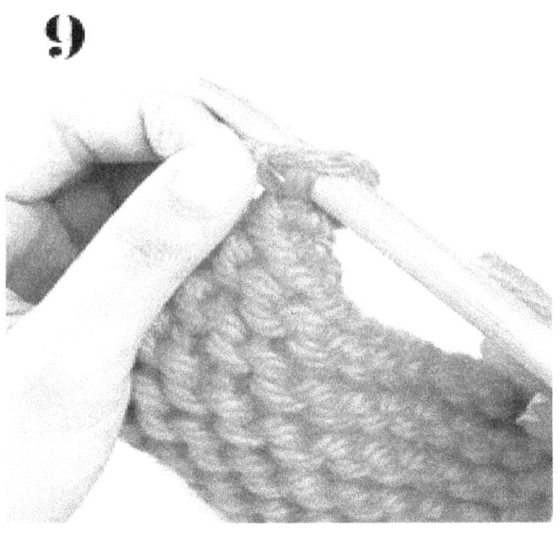

Pull the line over the yarn tail

10

Pull the yarn tail through the needle

11

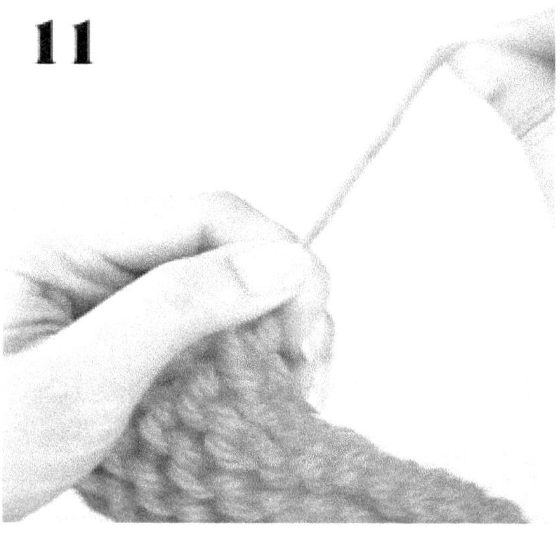

Pull the yarn tail to make it very tight

12

Your knitting is presently and safely off the needle!

And all done!

You're a Knitter!

CHAPTER FOUR

ESAY KNITTING PROJECTS FOR BEGINNERS

Easy steps on how to Knit a chunky Hat for beginners

Regardless of whether you're a starting knitter or a genius, you will adore how effectively this elegant cap knits up in the blink of an eye!

This example utilizes possibly weaves on a couple of 16" roundabout needles. Add that with some weighty wool, and you'll have yourself one attractive cap before you know it.

Stage 1: Materials

For a grown-up cap, I utilized 150g of massive wool, and one sets of size 10.5 16" round needles.

Extra apparatuses to make things simpler may incorporate a knit snare, a yarn needle, and a join marker, however you can likewise move away without these!

Stage 2: Swatch

Weaving a check sample is really
discretionary for this easygoing cap, yet in
case you're utilizing an alternate load of

yarn, you'll need diverse estimated needles, and well, it's simply a smart thought to understand what your completed item will match be!

So knitt yourself a 4" sq pattern. I like to begin and end my patterns with several lines of ribbing (k2, p2) so they don't twist up when you're set. The remainder of the pattern I do in stockinette. Notwithstanding, in case you're an expert and need to evaluate a pleasant example on this cap, practice that design in this pattern!

13" ↕
13" ↔ (on fold)
36 ÷ 3 = 12 ribs
$3\frac{1}{2}$ st/in

CO : 26 × 3.5 = 91

When you have your finished sample, you'll know the number of lines per inch your arrangement of yarn and needles will make, and you can sort out the number of fastens to project on!

For this cap, I needed it to go right around the hairline, rather than just around the center of my head. I wound up projecting on 72 lines to get the correct size. You may require less or all the more relying upon the size of your head and what your pattern advises you!

Truly, calculating this part is the hardest piece of your venture! Get the estimation you need for your cap, and increase it by the quantity of fastens per inch in your pattern. Presently go!

Stage 4: Cast On

I utilized the long-tail cast on technique. Since I generally utilize the long-tail cast on strategy. It's simply the one I recollect the most without any problem.

Being mindful so as to ensure none of your stitches are coiled (I do this by making the entirety of the nubby pieces point towards within and the entirety of the circles on the needles be outwardly), join your weaving by sewing into the primary fasten you made.

Stage 5: Ribbing

This progression is discretionary, and relies upon on the off chance that you need the edge of the cap to be ribbed or rolled.

For ribbing, work the cap in a Knit 2, Purl 2 for about an inch. I like to utilize a join marker to demonstrate where I began ribbing so I can stop at a similar point, however it's truly redundant.

For the edge to move up on itself, simply start in nonstop weaving.

Stage 6: get the Hat done!

Presently weave your heart out! Sew persistently until the cap estimates something you like. This one was sew to 13" from the edge of the edge. Quite floppy. On the off chance that you need it longer, sew more; more limited, sew less!

Stage 7: Finish

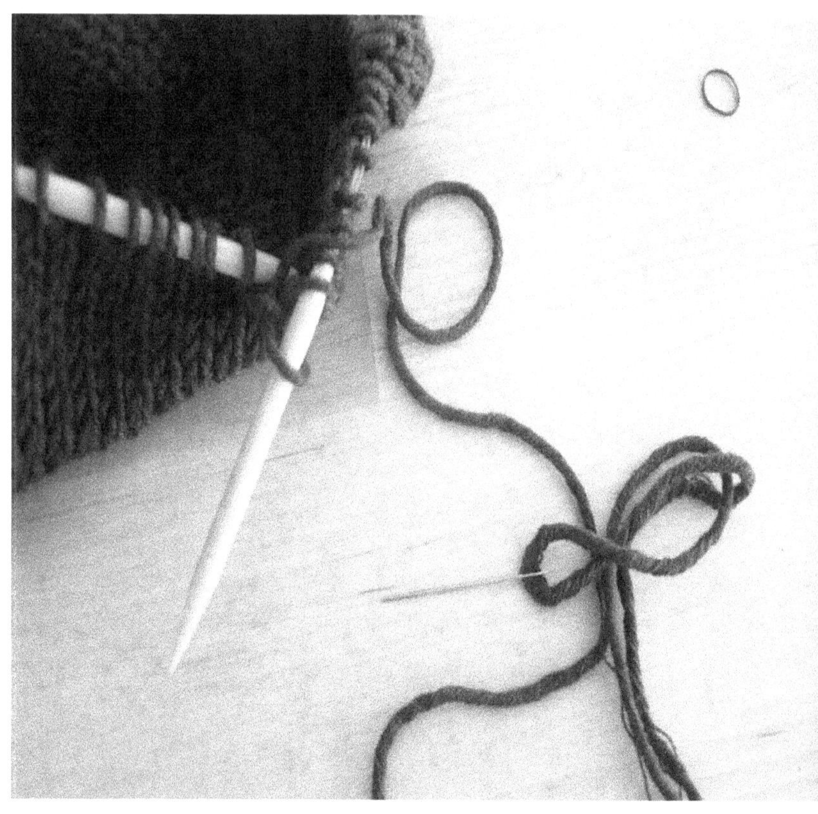

At the point when your cap is the length of
you like it to be, cut the yarn leaving a 12"
tail.

String the yarn through the entirety of the circles on the needle and pull tight (a yarn needle makes this stage a snap!)

Secure the finish of the yarn to within the cap, utilizing a bunch and weaving the end all through the sewing. You're finished!

This cap makes an extraordinary present for anybody in virus atmospheres. You can take the task anyplace with you and get weaving where you left off without recalling where you were in the example! It couldn't be simpler.

This cap is charming on anybody. It even obliges a head brimming with fears!

CHAPTER FIVE

EASY KNIT DISHCLOTH/WASHCLOTH

I've as of late become fixated on sewing dishcloths and washcloths. I've been exploring different avenues regarding making my own plans yet then idea I should have a go at something straightforward. This is an exceptionally essential sew dishcloth design that is incredible for amateurs. It doesn't need a great deal of weaving information to do and can be quite alleviating to make.

Give it a shot and see your opinion

Step 1: Supplies and Stitches

This is the least demanding dishcloth design out there and you're not going to require a lot to make it.

Supplies:

❖ Cotton yarn of choice - since this is a dishcloth/washcloth, you need 100% cotton, mercerized cotton should function also; both single and variegated shadings work for this example

❖ Knitting needles size 7 (sizes 5 - 7 should work, the end size of your washcloth will rely upon the needles you have, how close or free you need the fastens, and how thick or slender your yarn is)

❖ Counter (discretionary) - this can be useful with monitor join or columns. I didn't utilize it such a huge amount for this example, yet there are future examples I intend to make where this can be helpful to have

❖ Yarn Needle (not imagined)

stitches you need to know:

- Cast On (CO)

- Knit (K)

- Yarn Over (yo)

- Knit 2 Together (k2tog)

- Cast off (CO)

Step 2: Patterns

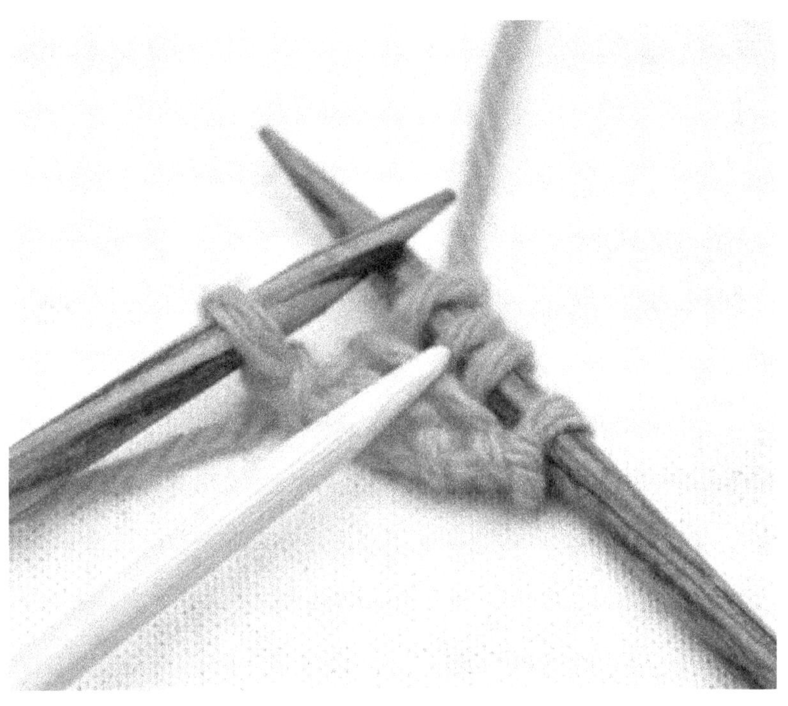

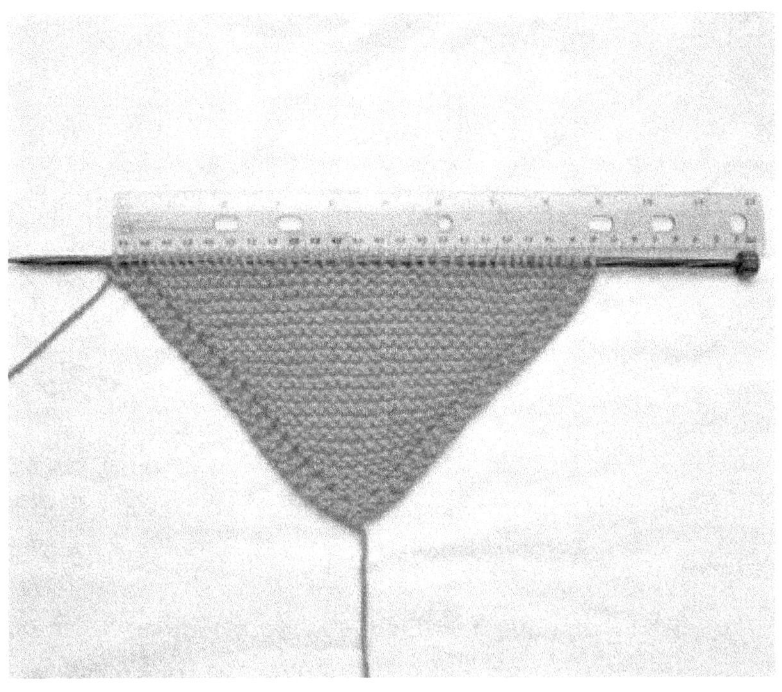

This example is quite simple. You just need to realize how to do a few columns and afterward you practically rehash the remainder of the time.

With the checks beneath, I wound up with a dishcloth that is about 6½"x6½". On the off chance that you need a greater one, simply keep on expanding until the sides are your ideal measurements.

Example:

1.   CO 4

2.   K 4

3.   K 2, yo, sew to end

Repeat stage 3 until you have 45 fastens across (or anyway numerous you need, it will rely upon your needles and yarn size, as you can find in the photos over, mine wound up having around a 9" askew with 6.5" sides).

4.   K 1, k2tog, yo, k2tog, weave to end

Repeat stage 4 until you are down to 4 join

At the point when you are done, just put the finish of the yarn through your last circle, fix it, and afterward shroud both your closures.

How this example functions is, each time you yarn over you are making that "opening" along the edge of the dishcloth while likewise expanding each line by 1 join.

The explanation you sew 2 together twice as you decline is so you can keep on doing the yarn over and proceed the "opening" line while likewise diminishing 1 join for each line.

Stage 3: Make them and Use them

Or on the other hand give them as
endowments. Everybody needs dishcloths
and washcloths.

CHAPTER SIX

HOW TO KNIT A SCARF FOR BEGINNERS

Numerous amateur knitters start with a scarf as their first task since the plan itself is basic. Deciding to make the scarf with an essential strap join makes it brisk and simple, yet at the same time a venture you make certain to be glad for when done. In the event that you know about projecting on, sewing, and official off, at that point you definitely know all you require to make a strap join scarf. On the off chance that you are new to weaving, all you require to know is here in this straightforward scarf design. You can even utilize the weave cast on and figure out how to sew as you get the fastens on your needle. It doesn't get any simpler!

In any event, when you are not, at this point a beginner knitter, a fastener line scarf is an extraordinary go-to design. It weaves up rapidly, and you get a serious diverse look with the littlest changes. You can add various surfaces, utilize different loads of yarn, work with more modest or greater needles, and make it thin or wide. The choices are boundless, even with a straightforward undertaking this way.

Get one skein of super-massive yarn (size 6 in the Craft Yarn Council's Standard Yarn Weight System), which ought to associate with 100 yards. Utilize two skeins in the event that you need a more drawn out scarf. The bigger the yarn and the lighter the shading, the simpler it will be to see your lines.

You will likewise require size 13 US (9 mm) sewing needles or whatever size makes the measure you need. It is likewise useful to have a knit snare. It is simpler to weave in the finishes of cumbersome yarn with a snare as opposed to a needle.

Example Gauge and Scarf Size

Measure discloses to you the number of lines there are per inch. It is influenced by the yarn weight, needle size, and your sewing pressure. With the recommended yarn and needle blend for this task, you ought to get around 2 1/2 fastens per inch in strap join.

In the case of changing yarn weight, you ought to likewise change the needle size to get that yarn's suggested measure.

The completed scarf is around 5 inches wide, yet the length will change contingent upon the yardage of your picked yarn and precisely how long you need to make it.

Strap Stitch Scarf Pattern

Sew this whole scarf design with a fastener join. It is just rehashing the essential weave join again and again. That is the reason it's the ideal amateur's undertaking! Before the finish of this scarf, you will have this sew join under control and be prepared to get familiar with the following fasten.

Materials Needed

Gear/Tools

Gear/Tools

- US 13 (9.0 mm) sewing needles

- M/13 (9.0 mm) sew snare for weaving in finishes

- Scissors

- 100 to 200 yards overly cumbersome wt yarn

Guidelines:

1. Cast On Stitches

Cast on 12 fastens. This will give you a scarf that is very nearly 5 inches wide, however you can adjust the quantity of fastens for a more extensive or smaller scarf.

There are a wide range of approaches to project on. Attempt the long-tail cast-on or basic wrap cast on.

2. Start Knitting

Sew each line and each line with a similar supporter join until you have about a yard of yarn left, or the scarf has arrived at your ideal length. You can likewise add another bundle of yarn to broaden the length or add an alternate tone.

3.   Bind Off Stitches

Next, you need to tie off. Cut the yarn, leaving a tail of around 6 inches.

4.   Finish

Utilize your stitch snare to weave in the closures at the top and the base, just as any additional finishes in the event that you added a second bundle of yarn. Square piece to get down to business lopsided fastens whenever wanted.

Make the Project Your Own

This universally handy scarf design is
amusing to make and simple to customize.
You can make it with any yarn type or join

two various types of yarn. In the event that you need to utilize an alternate load of yarn than the excessively massive, check the name to perceive what measure needles they suggest and use them rather than the size 13. You may likewise have to project on a couple of more join on the off chance that you are utilizing a lighter weight yarn to get a pleasant width—or you can make a super-thin scarf.

Modify your scarf with basic periphery at the finishes. Or then again add a couple of high quality pom poms on the corners or along the top and base.

When you have a couple of ventures added to your repertoire, you can sew a striped scarf with the extra pieces of yarn. An essential fastener line scarf is no uncertainty an undertaking you will continue to return to over and over all through your weaving profession. At the point when you are alright with strap join, figure out how to purl, and afterward you can attempt some stockinette projects also.

CHAPTER SEVEN

THE MOST EFFECTIVE METHOD TO MAKE A SPEEDY STOUT SEW CUSHION

utilizing yarn from your reserve – Get the thick look by weaving with a major needle and numerous strands of yarn from your reserve!

You gotta love a reserve buster example and this stout sew pad possesses all the necessary qualities. As much as we knitters love sewing, we likewise love gathering, storing, purchasing yarn quicker than we can sew with, consistently considering the best aims and examples. On the off chance that you have a yarn stash concealed away from your significant other, lift your hand here!

Materials needed.

- ❖ Bernat Softee Chunky Yarn, Glowing Gold, Single Ball

- ❖ Lion Brand Hometown USA Yarn (102) Honolulu
- ❖ Pink Patons Classic Wool Roving Yarn, Natural
- ❖ OXO Good Grips 100% Natural Cotton Twine, 300-Feet
- ❖ Lion Brand Scarf Knitting Needles, 19/15mm
- ❖ Fiskars 8 Inch Amplify Mixed Media Shears

© SMITHA KATTI
www.smilingcolors.com

To make these thick weave cushions I utilized yarns from my reserve and a size 19 sewing needles that make this a too speedy task. I didn't require an entire skein, pretty much a large portion of a skein of each should work for a pad. I am combining with 3 strands of yarn of different colors (one strand of every skein-a thick ochre yarn, a blue one and a strand of twine!) held together as one which brings about this beautiful t tweed-like surface and color.

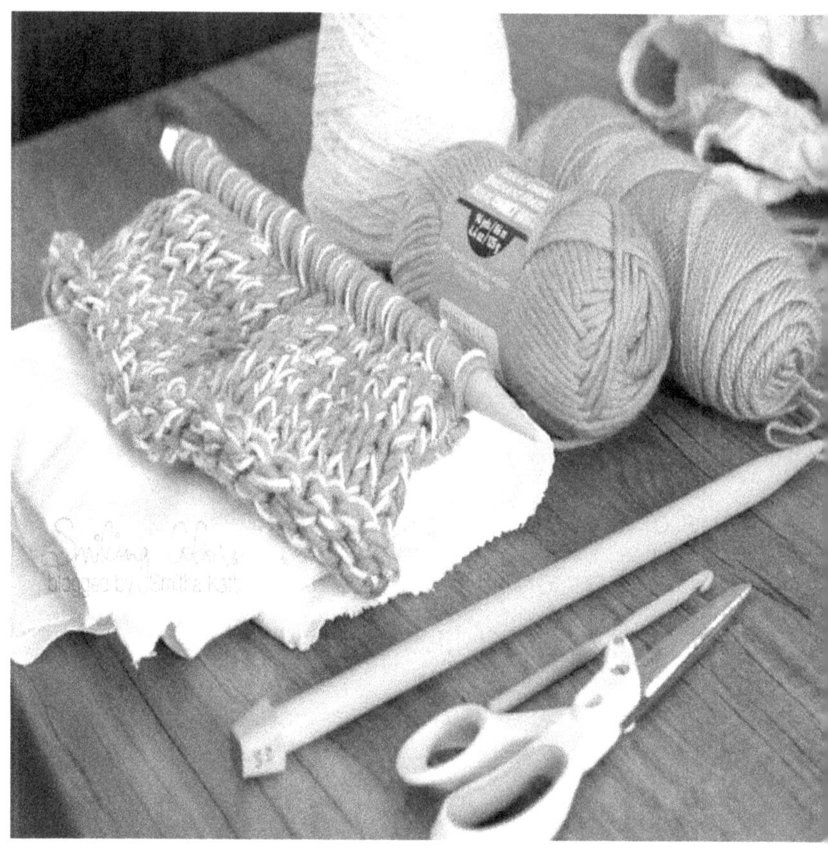

You will likewise require a knit needle, texture for the rear of the pads (my texture is really the abundance I remove the You will likewise require a sew needle, texture for the rear of the pads (my texture is really the overabundance I remove the lower part of our IKEA drapes) and a sharp pair of scissors.

step by step instructions to make it

Cast on stitch with three distinctive shaded yarns held together as one. I have done this sort of numerous strand sewing before in my Rainbow Knit Blanket Pattern and my Bulky weave cover free example yet I generally bent over a similar tone and sort of yarn. This time I increased my game and utilized triple strands and various yarns and one of them is in reality essential twine. I like how the dainty white twine separates the shading in the sew texture.

Sewing with numerous strands of yarn is an incredible method to accomplish a decent thick sew join. In any case, we don't have to go out and purchase a costly stout yarn for that, we are simply blending and coordinating yarns from our reserve itself. On the off chance that you might want a

monochromatic stout weave cushion
essentially utilize all strands of yarn from a
similar shading family.

Sewing the front of the cushion is simple as
it utilizes an essential Stockinette line. Cast
off when your necessary length is
accomplished.

I joined the sew pad fronts to the back
texture with a column of sew. This isn't the
best strategy I concur, however it turned out
consummately for me and was a snappy
alternate way.

What I did was cut little small openings around 1/4 inch inside from the edge of the texture. I cut each opening around 1/2 inch separated and afterward while going along with I embedded the sew guide into every one of these openings as I single sewed around. I was fortunate that the texture I picked didn't shred at the cut territories and that is a factor to note while picking your texture. On the other hand, you can simply weave 2 squares for every cushion one for the front and another for the back and consolidate them to cover the pad.

All done

The completed Chunky Knit pad looks incredible, however is so delicate and pretty to take a gander at. I am a major sucker for enormous stockinette fasten texture – thus I sew 3 of these pad covers. See the picture at the highest point of this post. I utilized a beige yarn for this cushion, a pink yarn for another design and a blue yarn for the last pad.lower part of our IKEA window